Practice Te...
for Key Stage 1

MATHEMATICS

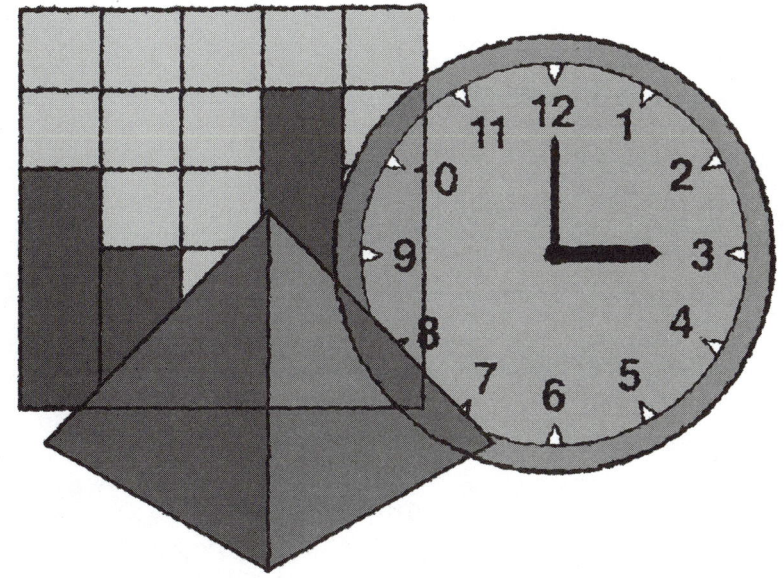

Peter Patilla

Oxford University Press

Acknowledgements
Many thanks to the editorial team at
Aldridge Press: Charlotte Rolfe, Maregold
Ofei, Sheila Dampney, Jocelyne and David.

Oxford University Press, Great Clarendon Street,
Oxford OX2 6DP

Oxford New York
Athens Auckland Bangkok Bogota Buenos Aires
Calcutta Cape Town Chennai Dar es Salaam
Delhi Florence Hong Kong Istanbul Karachi
Kuala Lumpur Madrid Melbourne Mexico City
Mumbai Nairobi Paris São Paulo Singapore
Taipei Tokyo Toronto Warsaw

and associated companies in
Berlin Ibadan

Oxford is a trade mark of Oxford University Press

© Peter Patilla 1997
First published 1997
Reprinted 1998 (twice)

ISBN 0 19 838200 6

Designed by Geoffrey Wadsley
Illustrations by John and Jane Booth
Packaged by Aldridge Press

Printed in Hong Kong

All rights reserved. No part of this publication
may be reproduced, stored in a retrieval system,
or transmitted, in any form or by any means,
without the prior permission in writing of Oxford
University Press. Within the U.K., exceptions are
allowed in respect of any fair dealing for the
purpose of research or private study, or criticism
or review, as permitted under the Copyright,
Designs and Patents Act, 1988, or in the case of
reprographic reproduction in accordance with the
terms of the licences issued by the Copyright
Licensing Agency. Enquiries concerning
reproduction outside those terms and in other
countries should be sent to the Rights
Department, Oxford University Press, at the
address above.

Contents

Using these tests	4
Practical task: Level 1	6
Test 1: Level 2	7
Test 2: Levels 2 to 3	16
Test 3: Levels 2 to 3	25
Test 4: Level 3	34
Answers	43
National Curriculum Record	47
Achievement Record	48

Using these tests

What are the Key Stage 1 Tests?

- In England, Wales and Northern Ireland all pupils aged between 6 and 7 must take a National Test in two subjects: English and Mathematics. The results of these tests will be reported back to parents.

- The National Curriculum is divided into Levels matched to ability. Level 1 is the starting point for children aged five, and Level 10 for very able sixteen year-olds. The average level reached by a child aged seven should be Level 2, although more able children will reach Level 3. Most children will be working at Levels 2 and 3 when they are aged six and seven.

- The National Curriculum tests for Mathematics at Key Stage 1 cover Level 1 as a practical task and Levels 2 to 3 as a written test.

How can these tests help?

- These tests have been designed for children aged six to seven, to help them prepare for assessment by the national tests. The questions in each test will give valuable practice for the National Curriculum tests and will give you information about how well a child is getting on with National Curriculum mathematics.

- The tests cover Levels 1 to 3 of the National Curriculum with particular emphasis on Levels 2 and 3.

- The mathematics work being tested in these tests covers Number and Algebra, Shape and Measures, and Handling Data and matches what is covered in the national tests.

- The chart on page 47 shows how each question relates to each of these three mathematical areas. It can also be used to show where a child needs more help and practice.

Using the practice tests

- There are 4 written tests with a short practical task at the beginning. This practical task is at Level 1 and if the child has difficulties with it then they might have problems with the remaining tests which are at Levels 2 and 3.

- Each of the tests 1 to 4 should take the child about 45 minutes to complete, but don't rush or pressurize them. Encourage them to do as much as possible but allow them to stop when they want to – remember that these are only practice tests.

- You can give some help to the child if they are unable to read the words in the question, provided this help does not extend to giving the answer or showing them how to reach the answer. The help should be confined to encouraging and reassuring them and confirming what they have to do.

USING THESE TESTS

About the practical task at Level 1
- Because this is a practical test you will need to give the instructions to the child. They should not be expected to read the instructions for themselves.
- Very simple practical apparatus will be needed for the test, as in the list below.
- If the child becomes tired or starts to lose concentration you may give the test in four parts, allowing time between each of the four questions.
- If the child can answer all the questions with confidence then they should be at or beyond Level 1 of the National Curriculum.

Materials needed
For the practical task:
- numbers 1 to 10 written on small pieces of paper, narrow strips of paper, 10 small objects for counting

For tests 1 to 4:
- pencil, centimetre ruler, small mirror

Instructions to the child
- Write the start and finish times on the test and work swiftly but carefully through the test.
- Look at the pictures and diagrams because they are part of the test and may help you.
- The questions get more difficult as you work through each test. Try all the questions but if you can't do one don't worry, just move on to the next question. At the end of the test go back, check your answers and have another go at any questions you found difficult the first time.

Marking the tests
- The answers are on pages 43 to 46.
- At the end of each set of answers is a guide to the mathematical level the child has achieved on that test.
- Encourage and reassure the child; confidence is an important factor when sitting for any test.

Finding the child's level
- An approximate level is found at the end of the answers to each test, and this gives an indication of how the child has done. A more accurate assessment can be obtained by adding the results of all the tests on the Achievement Record (page 48).
- This overall calculation will indicate whether the child has achieved Level 2 or Level 3 of the National Curriculum in these tests.
- It is important to remember that the national average is about Level 2. Any child reaching Level 3 is doing very well indeed.
- Use the chart entitled National Curriculum Record on page 47 as a guide to giving a child extra help. The chart shows both the level and the mathematical area being assessed.

Teacher assessment
Not all the mathematics work covered in schools as part of the National Curriculum is tested through pencil and paper tests. Teachers will use their experience and expertise to assess children in these areas and will add this information to the test results to give a final mathematical level for each child.

Practical task: LEVEL 1

Before Test 1 • Practical task at Level 1

You need 5 different strips of paper – all the same width.

Numbers 1 to 10 written on small pieces of paper.

10 counters such as beads, buttons, pieces of card.

1 The strips should be mixed up.
- Ask for the longest strip.

Show the child one of the strips.
- Ask the child to show a shorter strip.

The word 'longest' is what is being assessed.

The child can match different strips against the chosen one to find one which is shorter.

2 Choose the numbers 4 to 9 and mix up the order as opposite:

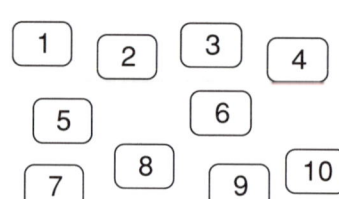

- Ask the child to put the numbers in order starting with the smallest number.

- Ask the child to choose the largest number and to match it with counters.

It does not matter whether the numbers go from left to right or go from right to left provided the child states which is the start number.

Do not say the number and only accept nine counters matched to number 9 as correct.

3 Choose the numbers ③ and ⑤.
- Ask the child to match each number with counters.
- Ask the child to find the number which matches how many counters there are altogether.

Only accept 8 as the right answer.

4 Choose the number ⑩
- Ask the child to match this with counters.

Choose the number ⑥
- Ask the child to take away this number of counters.
- Ask the child to find the number which matches how many counters remain.

Only accept 4 as the right answer.

Child has problems with any of the questions: working towards Level 1
Child correctly answers all questions with confidence: satisfactory Level 1

TEST 1 LEVEL 2

Test 1

Time started
Time finished

1

13 flowers in the garden.
7 of them are picked.

How many are left?

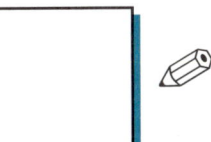

2 Write the total for this set of dice.

3 Write numbers in the shapes to add to 13.

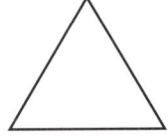 + 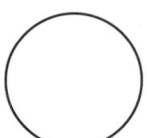 = 13

Here is a graph of some children's favourite vegetables.

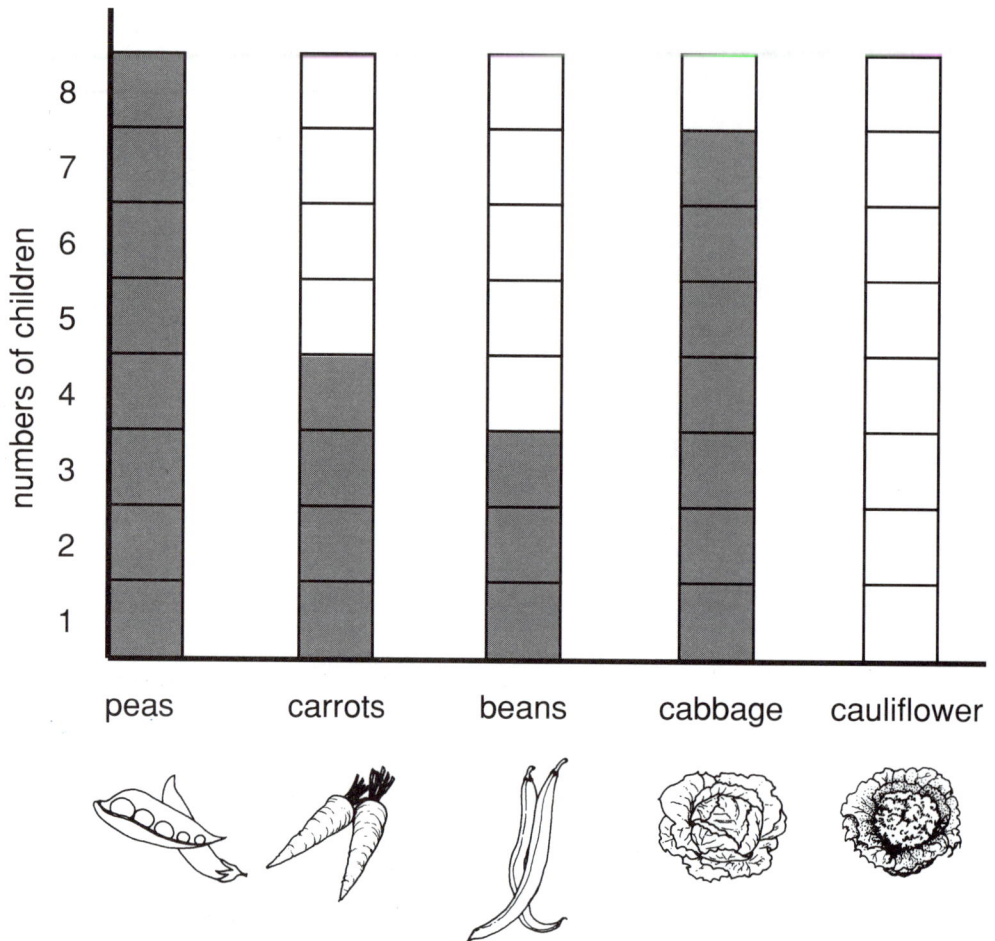

4 6 children liked cauliflower best.

Show this on the graph.

5 More children liked peas than beans.

How many more?

6 Lee has this amount of money.

How much has Lee altogether?

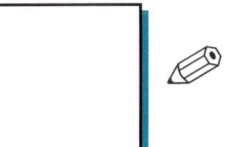

7 Write these numbers in order.

smallest

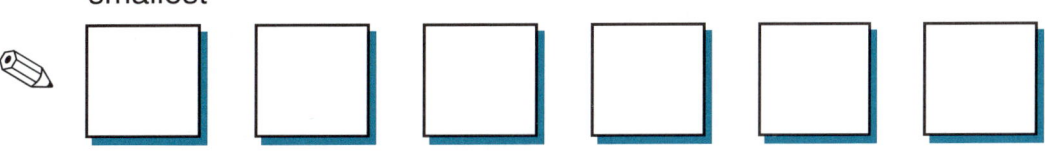

8 Tick the shapes which have only 4 straight sides. ✔

9 Which is the **longest** line? Measure it with a ruler.

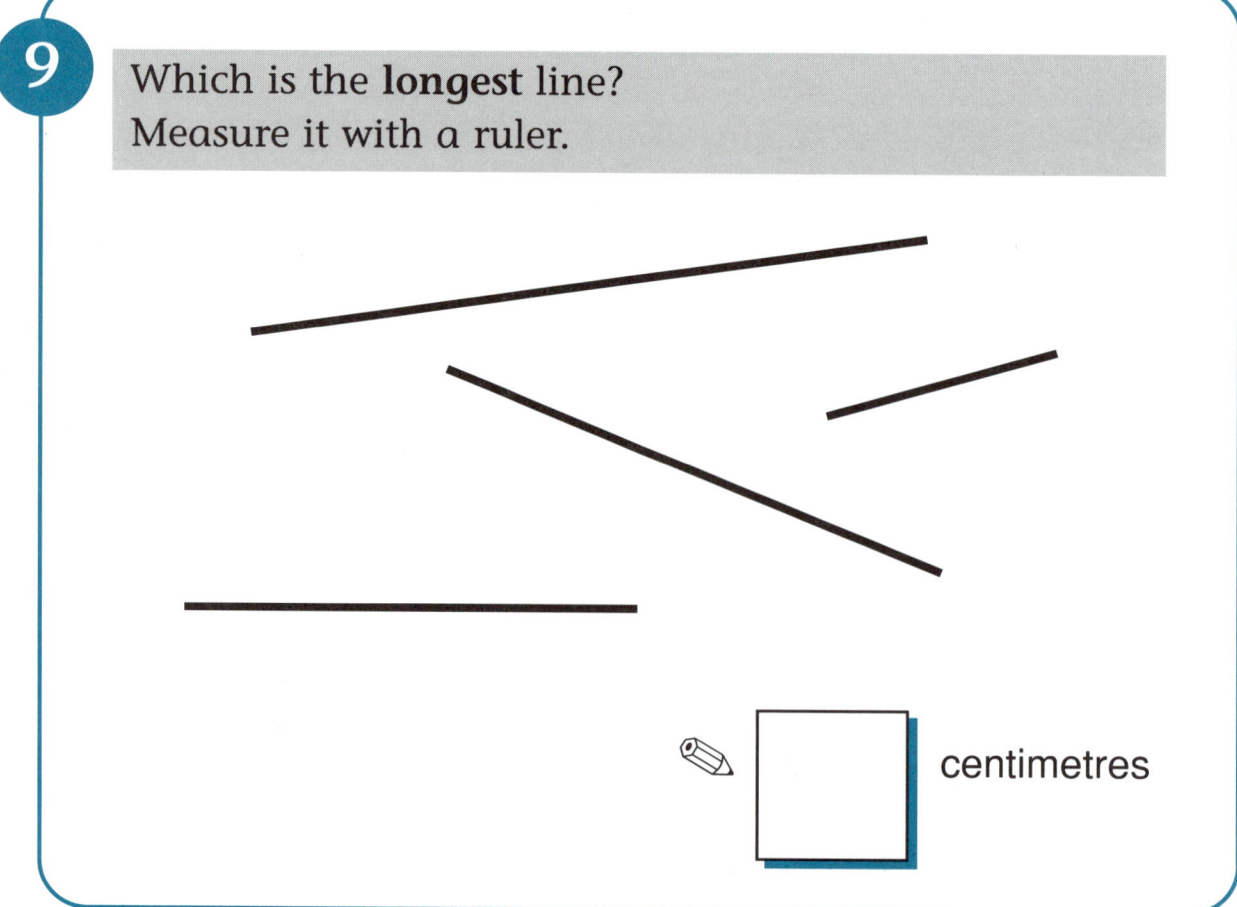

centimetres

TEST 1   LEVEL 2

10

Count the stars.
Colour **half** of them.

11 Write 3 **odd** numbers which are more than 30.

Children have sorted cards into four sets.

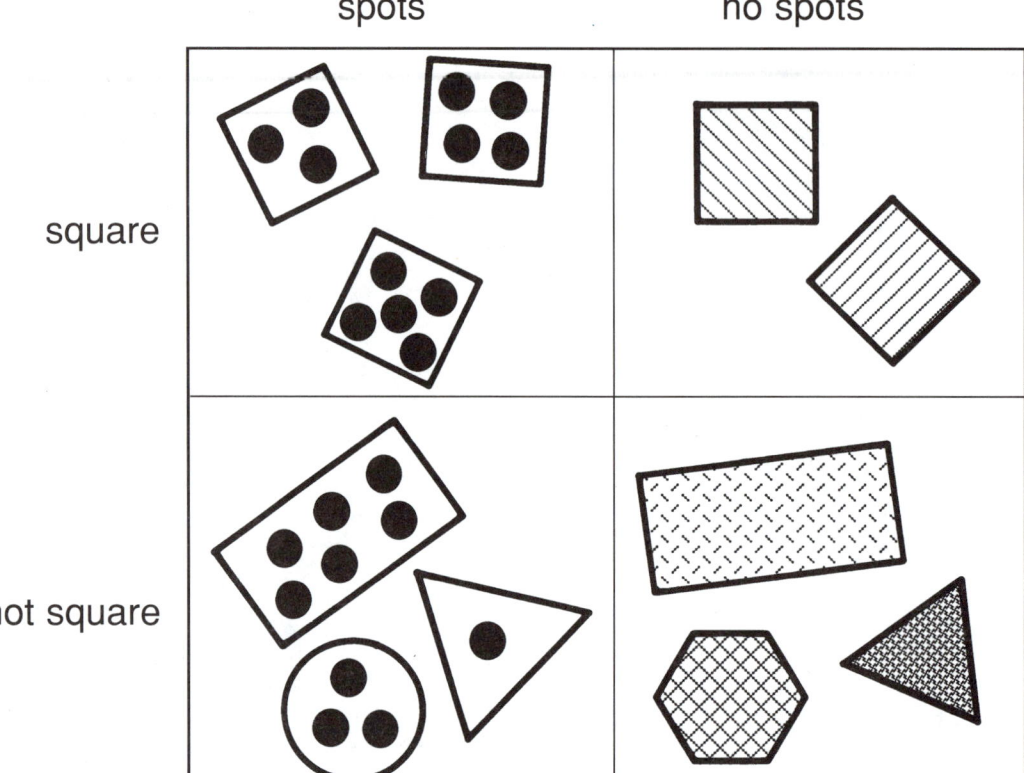

12 How many square cards altogether?

13 How many square cards without spots?

TEST 1 LEVEL 2

14 Join each shape to its name.

cylinder

cuboid

cube

15 This shape has turned through **one** right angle.

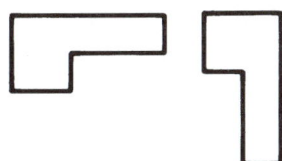

Tick which of these shapes have turned through **one** right angle. ✔

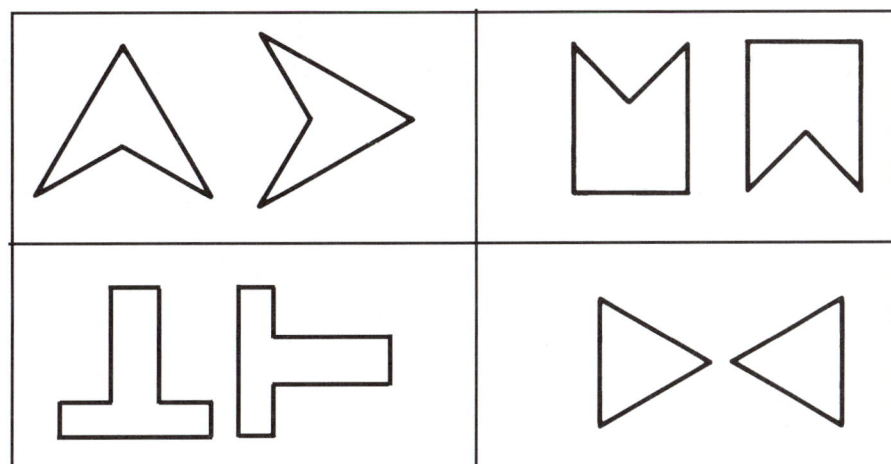

16 Finish this number pattern.

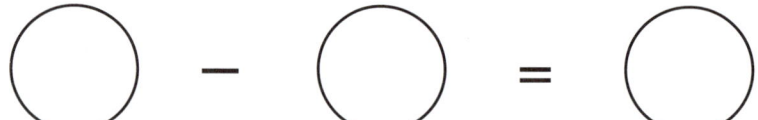

17 Join each shape to its name.

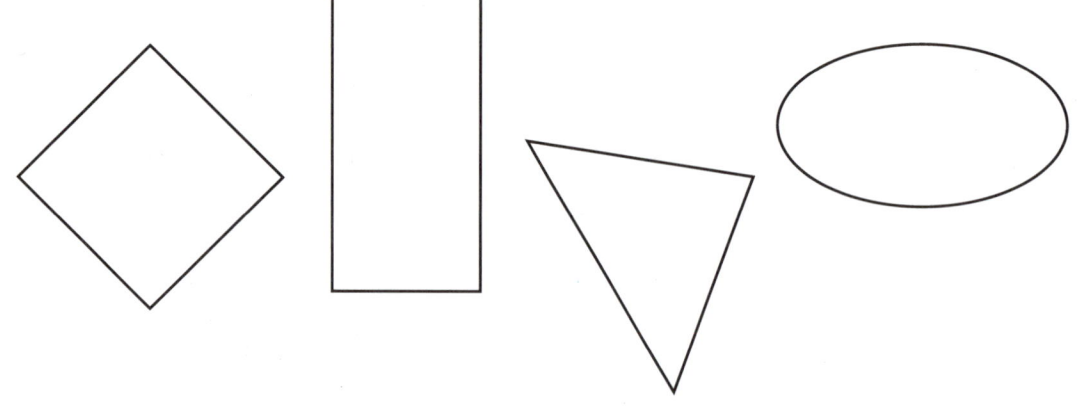

triangle   rectangle   square   oval

18 How many tens in 65?

19 Write in the missing number.

$\square - 3 = 7$

20 Join each sum to its answer.

(10 − 4)   (5 + 3)   (9 − 2)   (5 + 4)

8   6   9   7

TEST 2   LEVELS 2 to 3

Test 2

Time started
Time finished

1

5 children are joined by 6 more.

How many altogether?

2 Write numbers in the shapes to leave 6.

 − ◯ = 6

3 Here are some numbers.

20   19   18   17   16   15   14

Draw a circle round each **even** number.

4

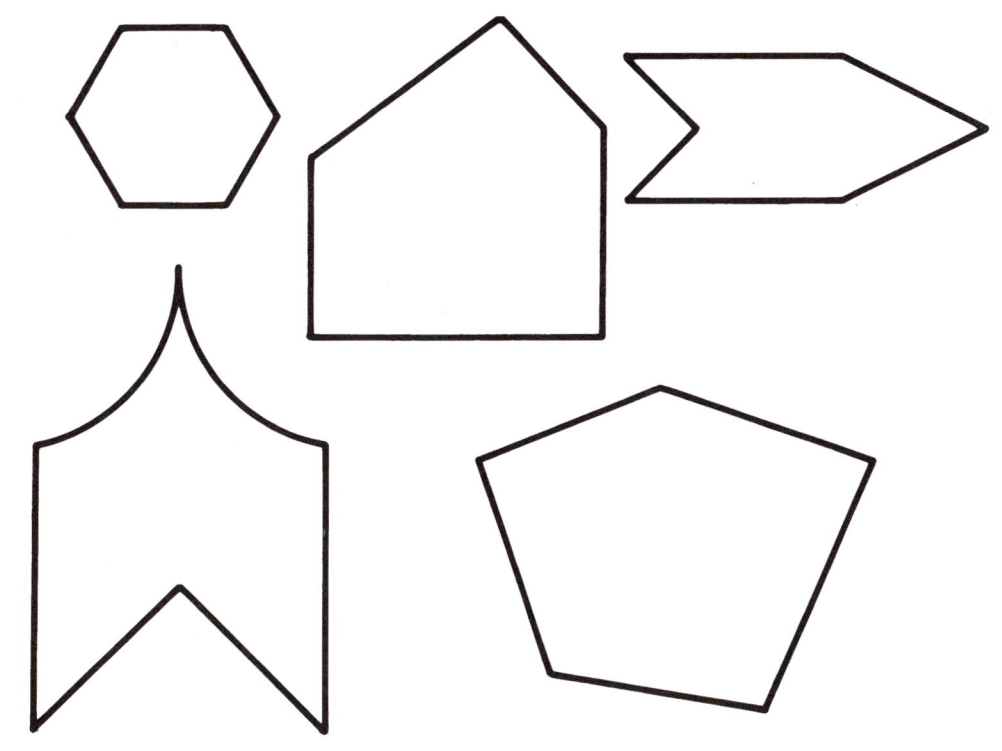

Tick two shapes which have **only** 6 straight lines. ✔

5

How long is this rope?
Measure it with a ruler.

 centimetres

These children all have pets.

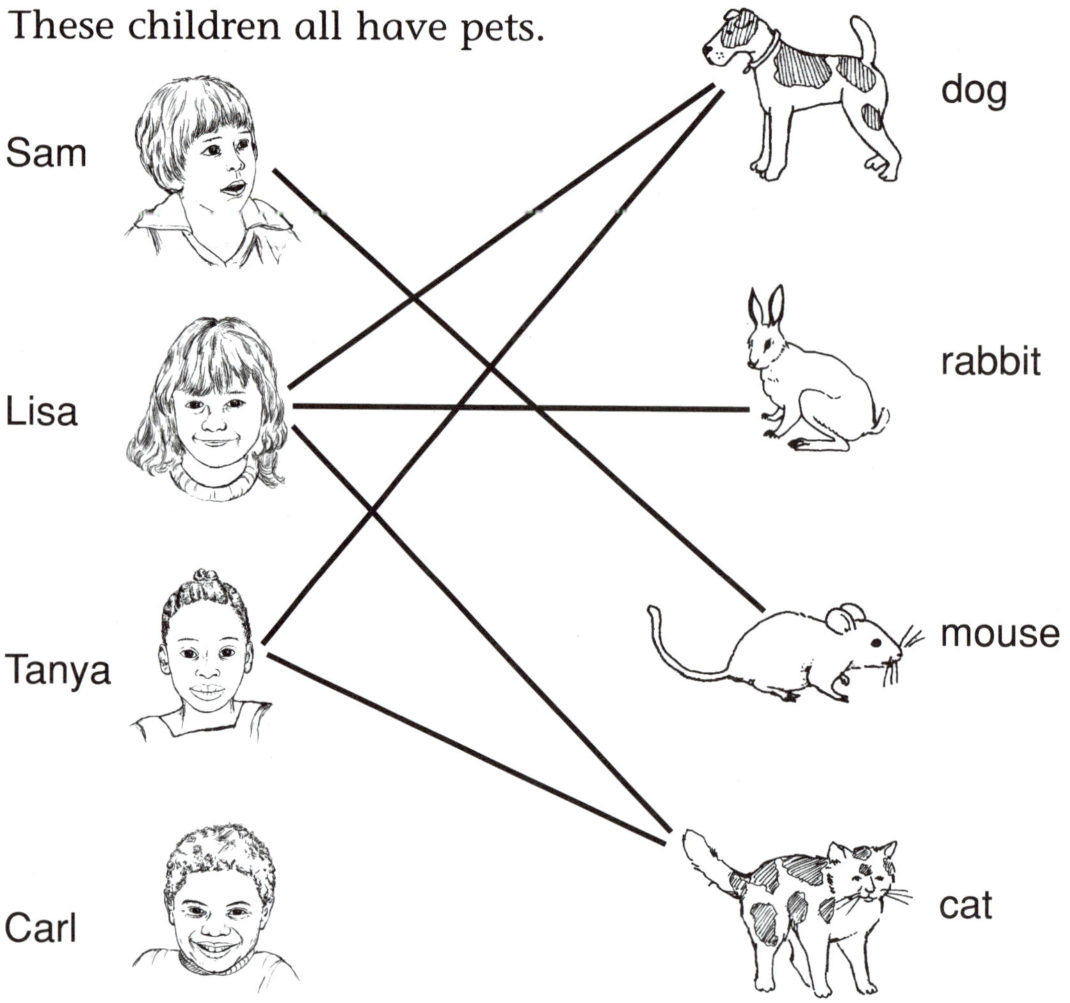

Sam — dog
Lisa — rabbit
Tanya — mouse
Carl — cat

(lines connecting children to pets)

6 Carl has a mouse as a pet.

Show this on the chart above.

7 Who has 3 pets?

8. Write in the missing number.

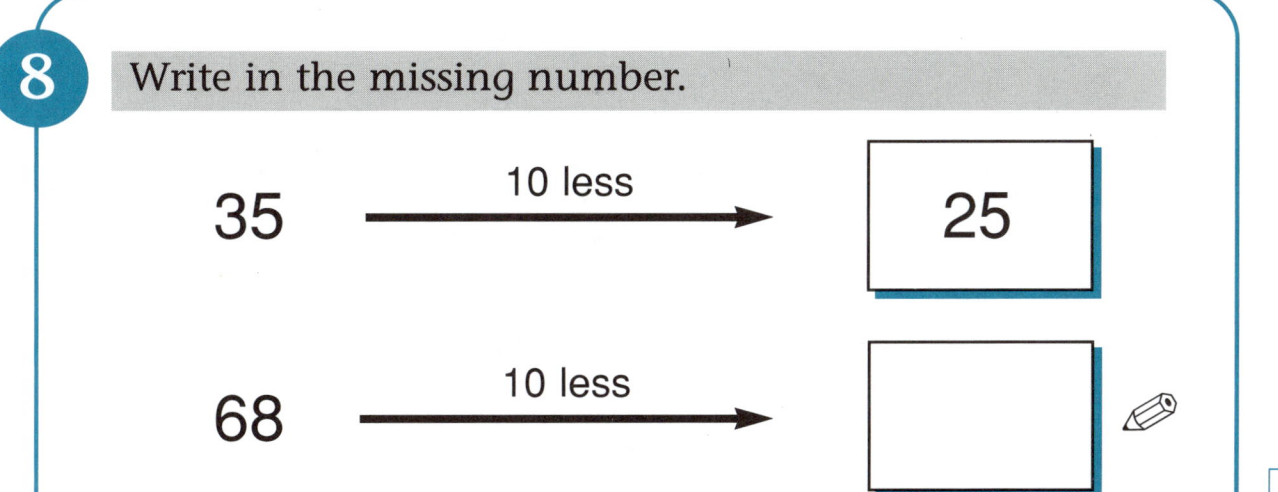

9. Write in the missing numbers.

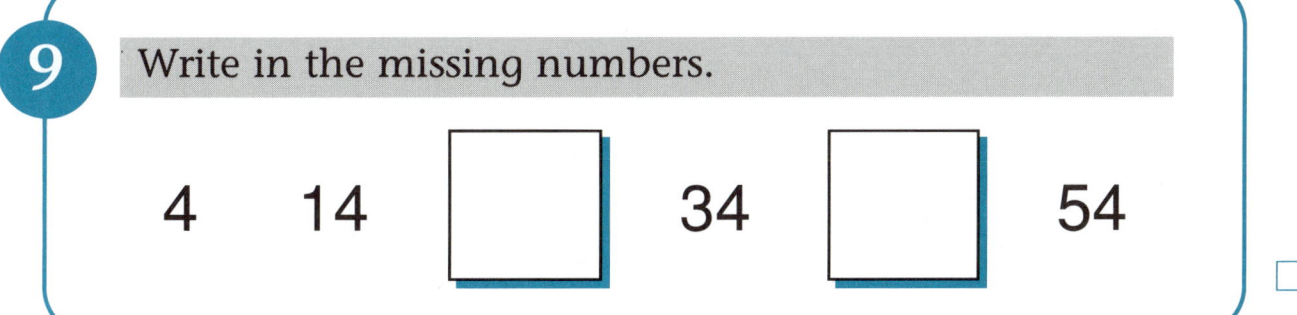

10. A fraction of each shape is shaded.

Tick the shape which shows $\frac{1}{4}$ coloured. ✔

11

teatime

bedtime

What time is bedtime?

12 Draw a ring round each cube.

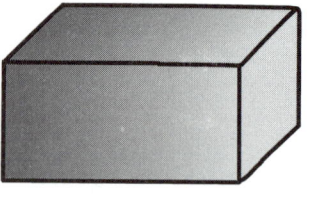 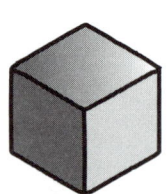 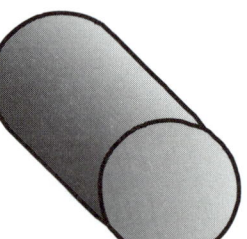

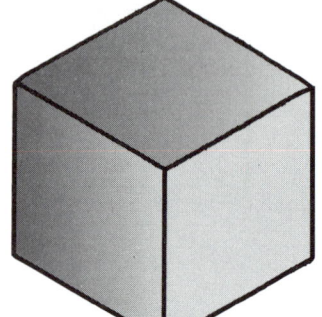 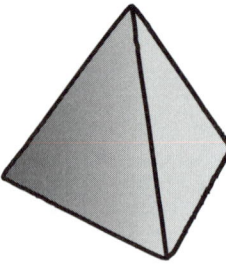 

13 Join each sum to its answer.

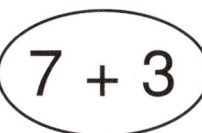  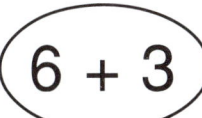

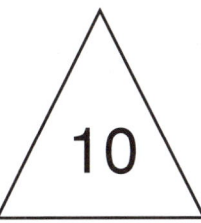 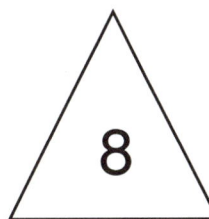 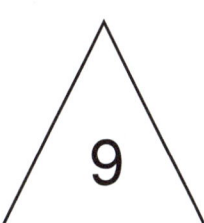 

14

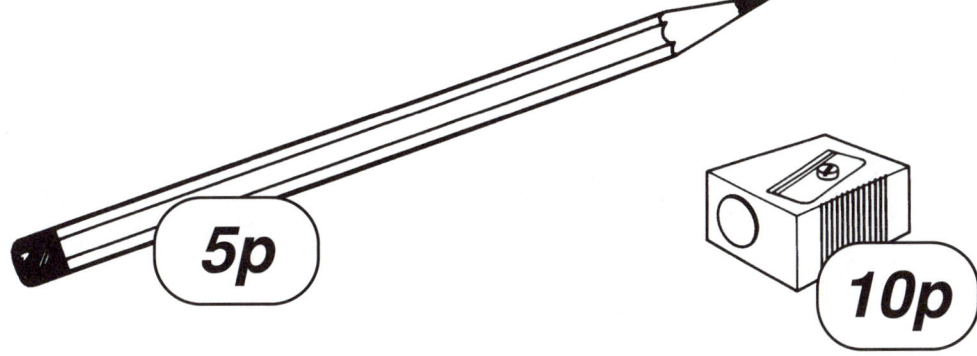

Fran buys both these.

How much change will she get from 20p?

 p

15 Join each picture to the right word.

kilogram

litre

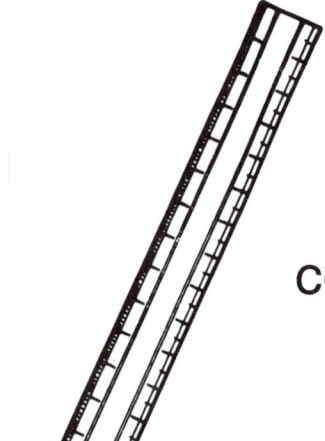

centimetres

minute

16 46 + 24 =

17 An egg box holds 6 eggs.

How many boxes are needed for 24 eggs?

 boxes

18 Here is a card.

Draw 2 lines of symmetry on it.

19 This graph shows the height of four tins.

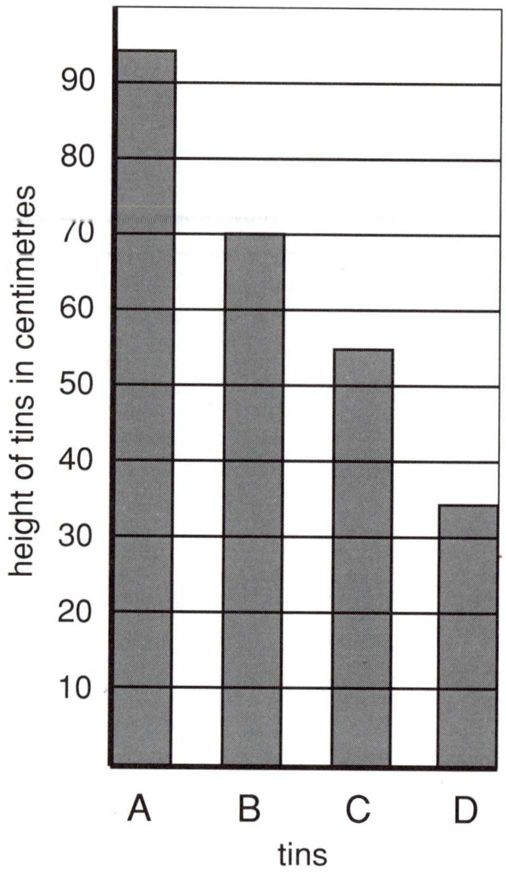

Which tin has a height of 55 centimetres?

tin ☐

20 Some of these numbers can be divided exactly by 5.

15   40   24   36   45   10

Write them here. ➡

can be divided exactly by 5

TEST 3   LEVELS 2 to 3

Test 3

Time started
Time finished

1 Here are some number cards.

8   4   3   6   7   5

Use **two** of the numbers to make 11.

 ☐ and ☐ make 11

2 How much money is there altogether?

  ☐ p

3 Here is a graph showing colour of eyes.

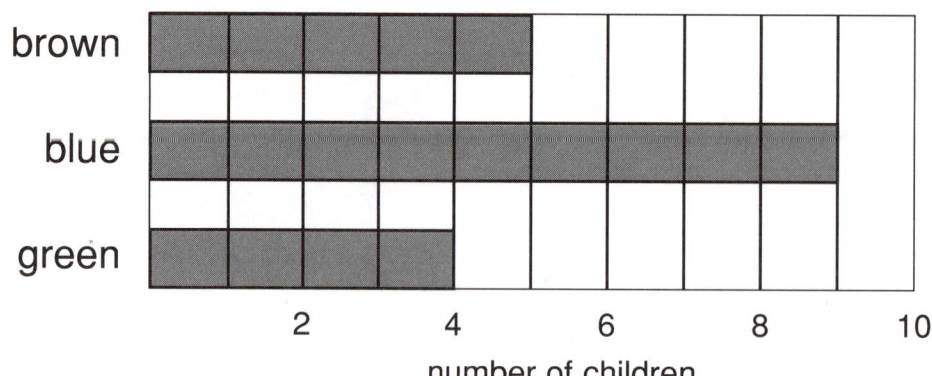

How many more children have blue eyes than brown eyes?

4 Some of these shapes are hexagons.

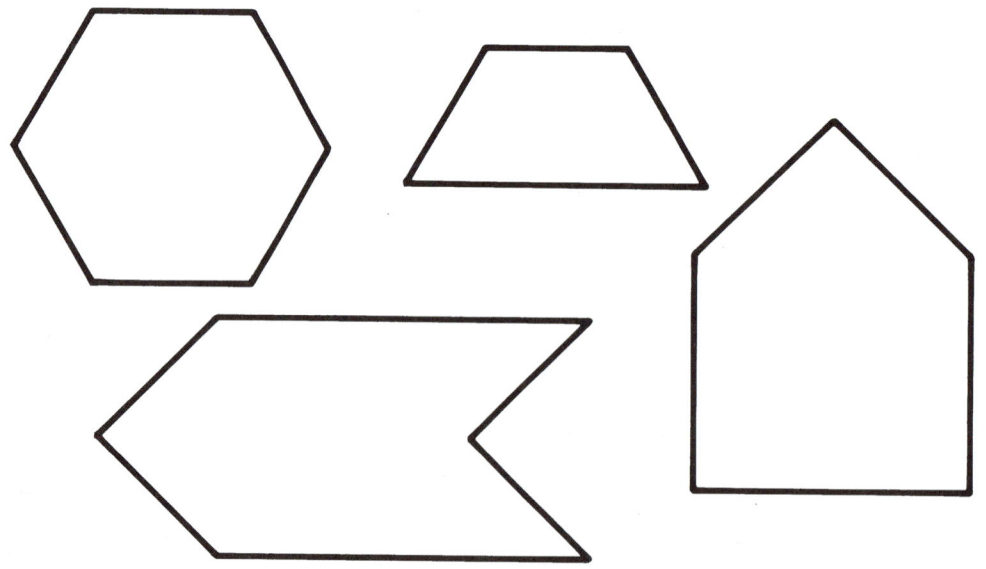

Tick each hexagon. ✔

5 Write in the missing number.

$$3 + \boxed{} = 8$$

6 Here is the start of a TV show.

The show lasts for 50 minutes.

What time does the show end?

7

$$69 - 45 = \boxed{}$$

8 Draw the reflection of this shape.

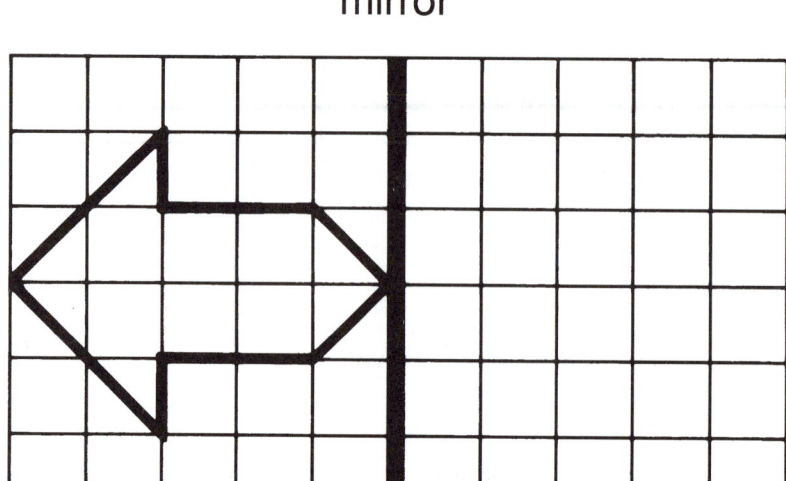

mirror

9 This table shows the comics read by some children.

comic	number of children
KIPPER	12
ZIG ZAG	8
FAB	5
HOBBIT	1
FUNTIME	7

How many more children read Kipper than Funtime?

10

ORANGE STICK
20p

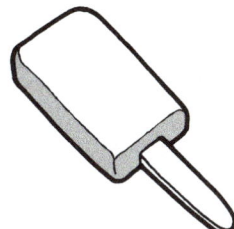
LEMON TWINKLE
25p

TASTE DELIGHT
30p

LIME SURPRISE
40p

Jo has 9p and wants to buy a TASTE DELIGHT.

How much more does he need?

p

11

What is the cost for 2 children?

£

The graph shows the number of visitors to school in one week.

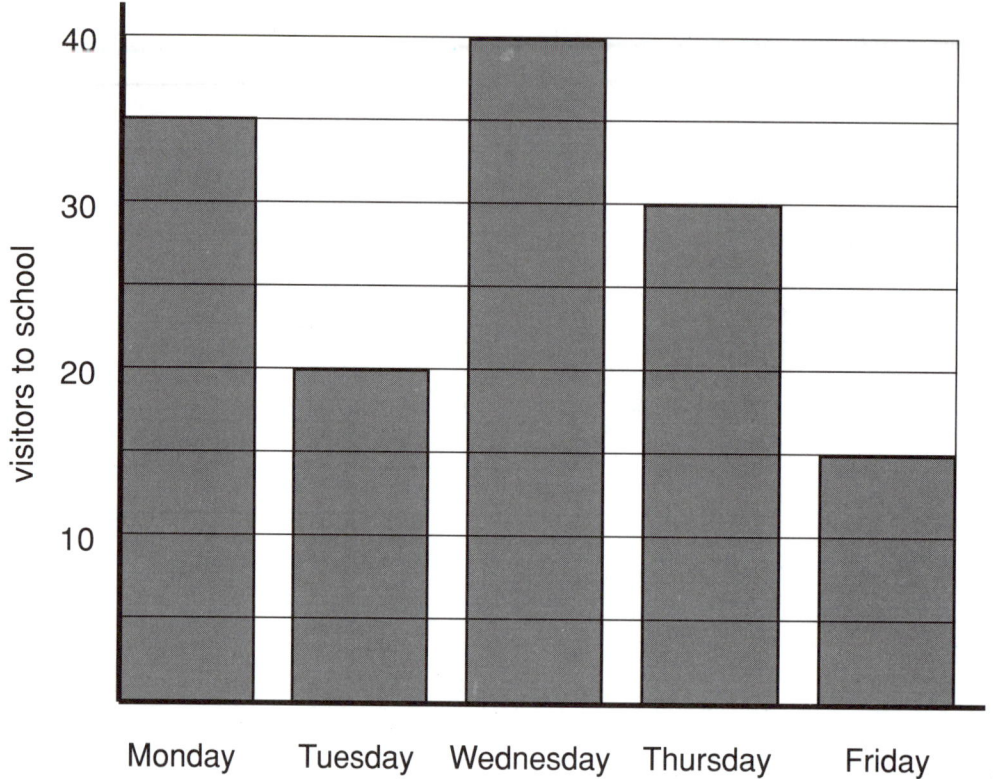

12 How many visitors on Monday?

13 On which day were there 30 visitors?

14

George — 99 cm

Alice — 61 cm

What is the difference in height between Alice and George?

☐ cm

15 Finish this number pattern.

56 —half→ 28 —half→ ◯ —half→ ◯

16 28 + 49 = ☐

TEST 3   LEVELS 2 to 3

17 This shape moves by a $\frac{1}{4}$ turn.

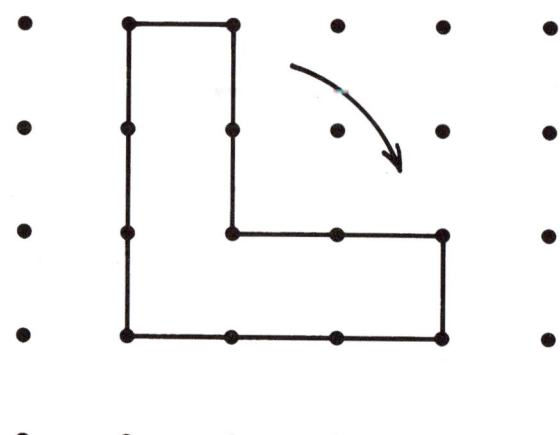

Draw what it looks like after the turn.

18 Write numbers in the shapes.

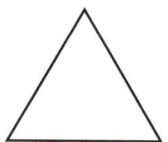 x 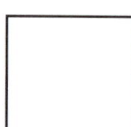 =  20

TEST 3   LEVELS 2 to 3

19 Write the temperature.

☐ °C

20 Draw a ring round all the numbers which can be divided exactly by 2.

16   54
    28
  17
        33
46
    50
        31

TEST 4   LEVEL 3

Test 4

Time started
Time finished

1 Write the missing number.

2 Tickets cost £5 each.

How many tickets can be bought for £33?

3 Lisa went to her gym club.

start   finish

How long did she stay?   minutes

4 One of these shapes does not have reflective symmetry.

Put a cross in the shape. ✗
Use a mirror to help.

5 Use a ruler.

How much longer is the shaded straw?

 centimetres

6 87 − 34 = ☐

7 Here are 3 numbers.

9   8   17

Use **these** numbers to finish each sum.

9 + 8 = 17

☐ + 9 = ☐

☐ − 8 = ☐

☐ − ☐ = 8

This graph shows the numbers of people who visited a sports centre in one week.

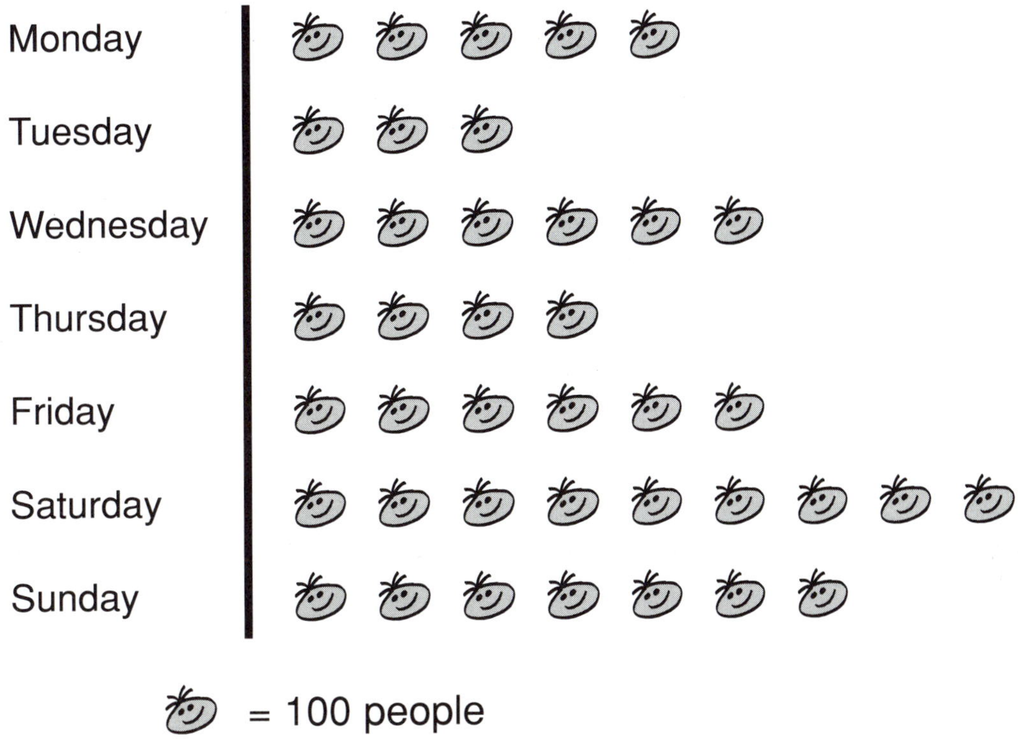

Day	Visitors
Monday	🙂 🙂 🙂 🙂 🙂
Tuesday	🙂 🙂 🙂
Wednesday	🙂 🙂 🙂 🙂 🙂 🙂
Thursday	🙂 🙂 🙂 🙂
Friday	🙂 🙂 🙂 🙂 🙂 🙂
Saturday	🙂 🙂 🙂 🙂 🙂 🙂 🙂 🙂 🙂
Sunday	🙂 🙂 🙂 🙂 🙂 🙂 🙂

🙂 = 100 people

8 On which day did 900 people visit the centre?

9 How many people visited on Saturday and Sunday?

10 39 + 46 = ☐

11

	even numbers	odd numbers
numbers less than 100	48	
numbers greater than 100		

Write in one possible number in each empty box.

12 Write these numbers in order.

776   345   435   306   676

smallest
☐ ☐ ☐ ☐ ☐

13 Turn this shape $\frac{1}{4}$ turn clockwise.

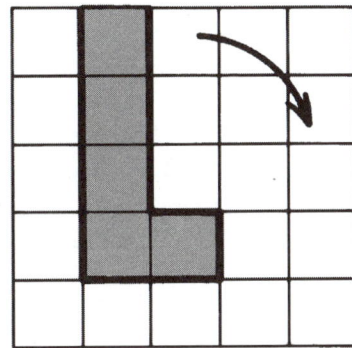

Draw it on the grid.

 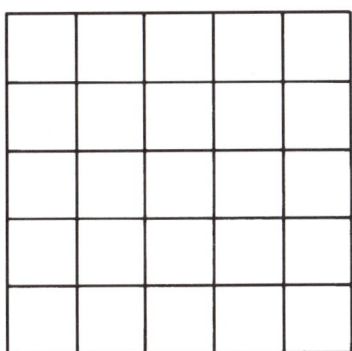

14 Which of these numbers is nearest to three hundred and fifty? Tick it. ✔

450	
340	
400	
380	

TEST 4   LEVEL 3

15 How many 2p coins can you get for 50p?

16 These shapes have been sorted.
One shape is in the wrong place.

straight edges   curved edges

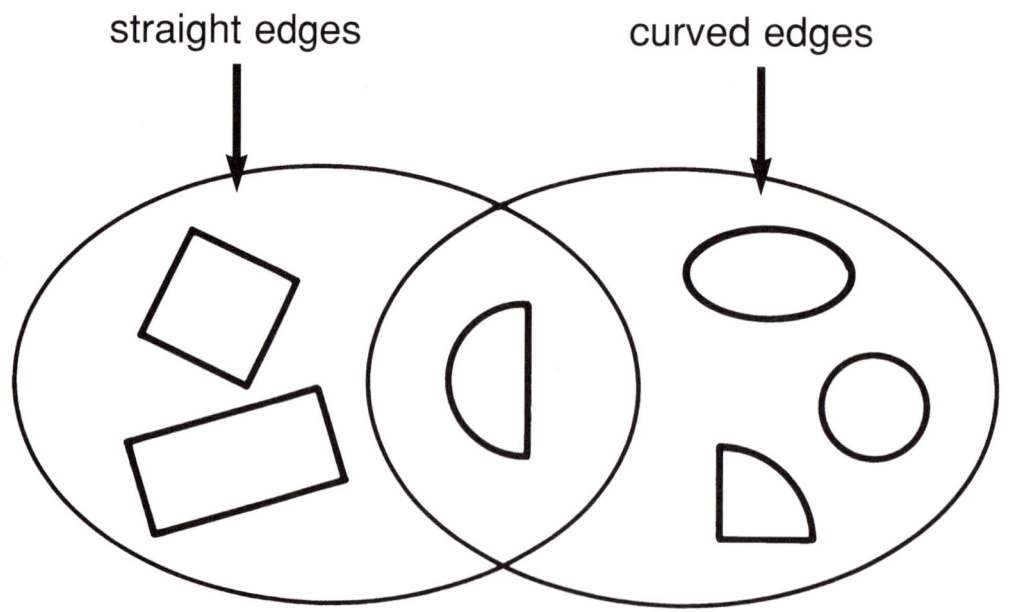

Mark the shape which is wrong.   ✗

Here is a timetable for a school's PE lessons.

	Mon	Tue	Wed	Thu	Fri
10.00 – 10.30	class 1	class 3	class 6	class 2	class 4
10.30 – 11.00	class 5	class 7		class 8	
1.30 – 2.00	class 6	class 1	class 4		class 7
2.00 – 2.30	class 2	class 8	class 3		class 5

17 Which class has PE on Tuesday between 2.00 and 2.30?

18 On which 2 days do class 5 have PE?

TEST 4   LEVEL 3

19 What is the total cost of **five** books which cost £5 each?

£

20 Complete this number pattern.

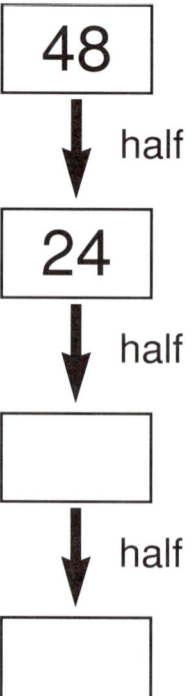

TEST 1 Level 2

• Answers to Test 1 •

1 6

2 14

3 △ + ◯ = 13
Any two numbers which add up to 13 are correct.

4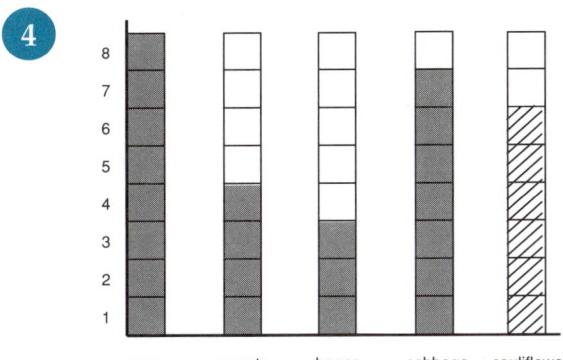

5 5

6 30p

7 13 31 42 60 87 94

8
both shapes must be ticked

9 9 centimetres

10 Only 4 stars should be coloured

11 Any 3 odd numbers more than 30, e.g. 31, 39, 45, 57, 93

12 5

13 2

14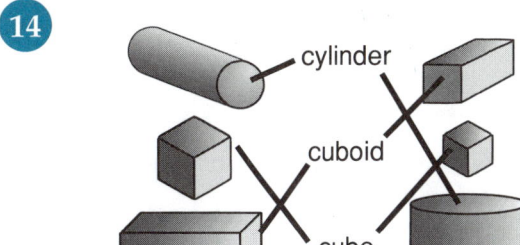

15

16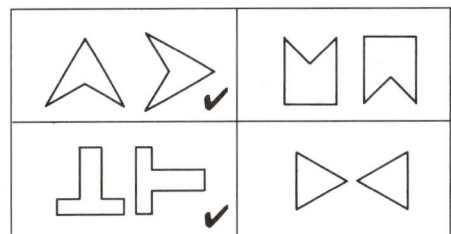

17 triangle rectangle square oval

18 6

19 10

20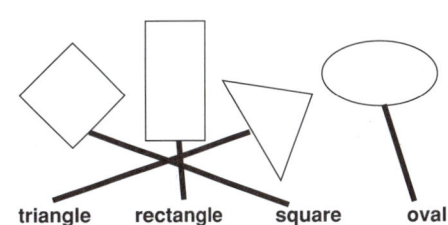

TEST 1
5 – 13 questions correct — working towards Level 2 standard
14 – 17 questions correct — satisfactory Level 2 standard
18 – 20 questions correct — good Level 2 standard

Answers to Test 2

TEST 2   Levels 2 to 3

1. **11**

2. △ + ○ = 6
   Any two numbers which when taken away leave 6

3. ⑳ 19 ⑱ 17 ⑯ 15 ⑭

4. (hexagon ✓, arrow ✓)

5. **9** centimetres

6.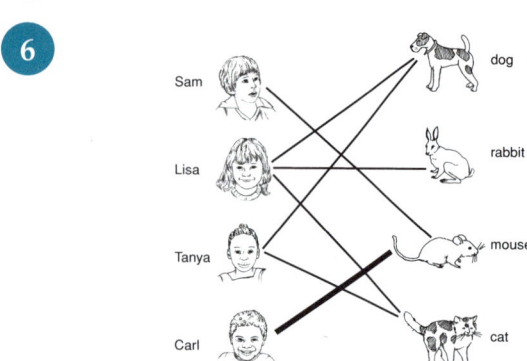

7. **Lisa**

8. **58**

9. 4 14 **24** 34 **44** 54

10. (square with cross ✓)

11. **9 o'clock or 9.00.**

12.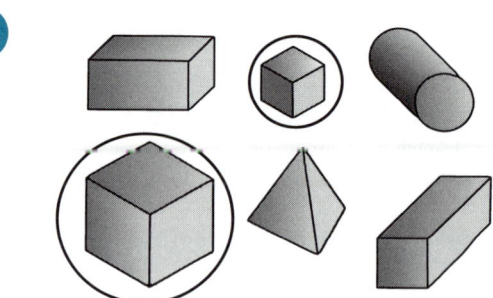

13. 7 + 3 → 10; 10 − 3 → 7; 9 − 1 → 8; 6 + 3 → 9

14. **5p**

15.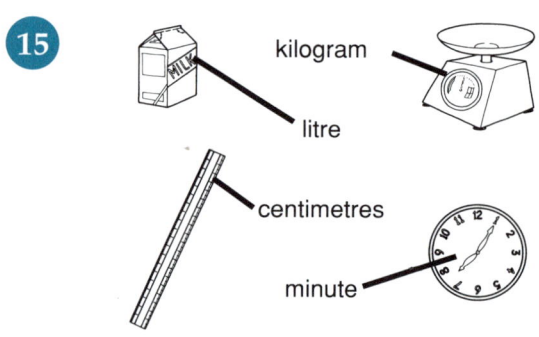

16. **70**

17. **4** (boxes)

18. (diamonds completing symmetry)

19. **C**

20. can be divided exactly by 5
    15   45
       40
          10

    All 4 numbers must be correct.

TEST 2

8 – 11 questions correct   working towards Level 2
12 – 15 questions correct   satisfactory Level 2 standard
16 – 20 questions correct   good Level 2 standard, some Level 3

Answers to Test 3

TEST 3 Levels 2 to 3

1. **8 & 3** *or* **3 & 8** *or* **4 & 7** *or* **7 & 4** *or* **6 & 5** *or* **5 & 6**

2. **25**p

3. **4**

4.

   Both must be ticked.

5. **5**

6. **9:20**

7. **24**

8.

9. **5**

10. **21**p

11. **£1.30** *not* **130** *or* **130p** *or* **1.30p**

12. **35**

13. **Thursday**
    (Monday and Wednesday would also be acceptable.)

14. **38** centimetres

15.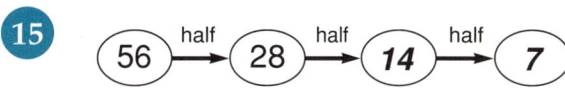

16. **77**

17.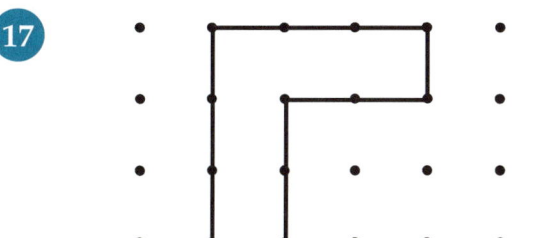

18. **4 & 5** *or* **5 & 4** *or* **2 & 10** *or* **10 & 2** *or* **1 & 20** *or* **20 & 1**

19. **60**°C

20. ⓘ6   ㉘   17   33   ㊻   ㊿   54   31

    All 5 numbers must be ringed.

TEST 3

5 – 11 questions correct	good Level 2 standard, some Level 3
12 – 15 questions correct	working towards Level 3
16 – 20 questions correct	satisfactory Level 3

Answers to Test 4

1 399

2 6 tickets

3 45 minutes

4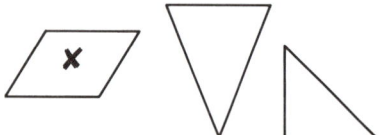

5 6 centimetres

6 53

7
9	+	8	=	17
8	+	9	=	**17**
17	−	8	=	**9**
17	−	**9**	=	8

8 Saturday

9 1600 people

10 85

11
	even numbers	odd numbers
numbers less than 100	48	any **odd** number which is **less** than 100 is correct
numbers greater than 100	any **even** number which is **more** than 100 is correct	any **odd** number which is **more** than 100 is correct

12 306 345 435 676 776

13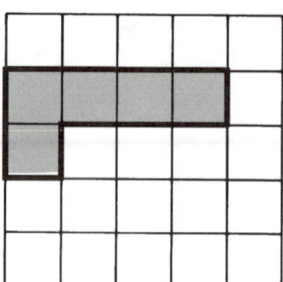

14
450	☐
340	✔
400	☐
380	☐

15 25

16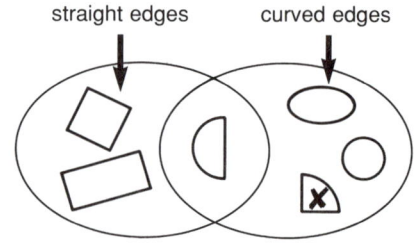

17 class 8

18 Monday and Friday

19 £25

20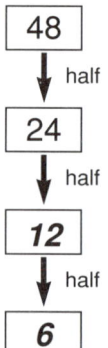

TEST 4

5 – 13 questions correct working towards Level 3 standard
14 – 17 questions correct satisfactory Level 3 standard
18 – 20 questions correct good Level 3 standard

National Curriculum Record

	Level 2			Level 3				Level 2			Level 3		
	Number & Algebra	Shape & Measures	Handling data	Number & Algebra	Shape & Measures	Handling data		Number & Algebra	Shape & Measures	Handling data	Number & Algebra	Shape & Measures	Handling data
TEST 1							**TEST 3**						
1	■						1	■					
2	■						2	■					
3	■						3		■				
4			■				4		■				
5		■					5	■					
6	■						6					■	
7	■						7				■		
8		■					8				■	■	
9		■					9						■
10	■						10				■		
11	■						11				■		
12			■				12					■	
13	■						13				■		
14		■					14				■		
15	■						15					■	
16	■						16				■		
17		■					17				■		
18	■						18				■		
19	■						19						■
20	■						20						
TEST 2							**TEST 4**						
1	■						1				■		
2	■						2				■		
3	■						3					■	
4		■					4				■		
5	■						5				■		
6			■				6				■		
7	■						7				■		
8	■						8						■
9	■						9				■		
10	■						10				■		
11			■				11				■		
12		■					12				■		
13	■						13					■	
14	■						14				■		
15		■					15					■	
16					■		16					■	
17					■		17						■
18					■		18						■
19					■		19					■	
20				■			20				■		

Using this Record

Check the answers for each of the tests. If an answer is wrong, put a cross in the tinted box beside the question number.

Look at where the crosses are and see where help is most needed in National Curriculum mathematics – and at what Levels.

Achievement Record

Write the score out of 20 for each test.

Mark the grand total out of 80 on the Achievement Record line. This gives an overall Level for the four tests.

TEST 1 ☐

TEST 2 ☐

TEST 3 ☐

TEST 4 ☐

GRAND TOTAL ☐

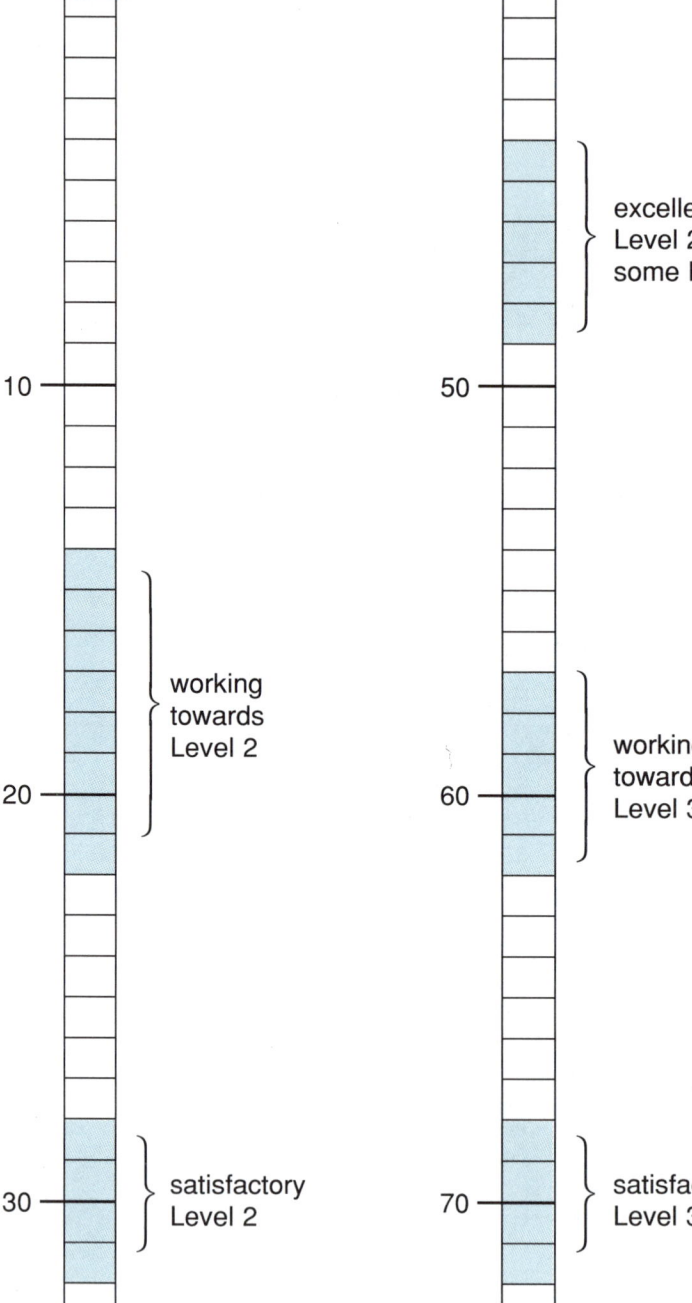